Want to Know

Robert Pattinson

 BY KAY BARNHAM

WAYLAND

First published in 2013 by Wayland
Copyright © Wayland 2013

Wayland
338 Euston Road
London NW1 3BH

Wayland Australia
Level 17/207 Kent Street
Sydney, NSW 2000

Commissioning editor: Debbie Foy
Designer: Alyssa Peacock & Lisa Peacock
Series editor: Camilla Lloyd

Dewey ref: 791.4'3'028'092-dc23
ISBN: 978 0 7502 7933 8
10 9 8 7 6 5 4 3 2 1

Printed in UK
Wayland is a division of Hachette Children's Books,
an Hachette UK company

www.hachette.co.uk

The author and publisher would like to thank the following for
allowing their pictures to be reproduced in this publication: Cover
and 4 © Joe Stevens./Retna Ltd./Corbis; 8 © PAUL BUCK/epa/Corbis;
17 © MARIO ANZUONI/Reuters/Corbis; 23 © SEBASTIEN NOGIER/
epa/Corbis; 32 © Stephane Cardinale/People Avenue/Corbis; 35 © Kurt
Krieger/Corbis; 58 © MARIO ANZUONI/Reuters/Corbis; 63 © Frank
Trapper/Corbis; 66 © ALEJANDRO GARCIA/epa/Corbis; 78 © Splash
News/Splash News/Corbis.

This book is not affiliated with or endorsed by Robert Pattinson.

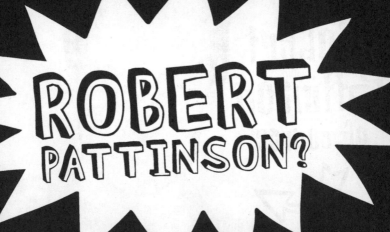

Want to know
EVERYTHING
there is to
know about

ROBERT
PATTINSON?

Then head this way...

HE'S THE MOST FAMOUS VAMPIRE ON THE PLANET. HE'S AN AWESOME WIZARD, A WORLD FAMOUS SPANISH PAINTER, A CIRCUS RUNAWAY AND A TROUBLED NEW YORKER ... AND BY THE TIME YOU READ THIS, HE MAY HAVE BEEN A STACK OF OTHER CHARACTERS, TOO. BECAUSE HE'S ALSO ONE OF THE HOTTEST ACTORS IN HOLLYWOOD

SO WHO IS HE?

He's Robert Pattinson, of course.

If you're reading this, then you must already be one of RPattz's fans. But how much of a **SUPER-FAN** are you? Do you know everything there is to know about your idol? Are you sure? Do you know what colour his eyes are when he's not being a vampire? How tall is he? What instruments can he play? Did he **REALLY** adopt a dog and fly it to Los Angeles on a private jet?

This book tells you **EVERYTHING** you need to know about Robert Pattinson. Right now, you're just a few pages away from becoming one of his **biggest fans** ever. And there's more. Armed with your new stack of facts, you'll also get to prove your **über-fan** status by scoring top marks in the fiendishly difficult quizzes dotted throughout the book.

WANT TO KNOW YOUR IDOL?

All you have to do is turn the page...

Robert Douglas
Thomas Pattinson was born on
13 May 1986 in Barnes, south-west
London. He went to school like
any normal kid until he was 12, and
that's when things started to get
just a little bit glitzy for the London
lad because he became a **model**.

Ooooh!

It didn't last, though. After four years of modelling, the work dried up. But this turned out to be a good thing. Robert joined the Barnes Theatre Company, appearing in stage productions of **Tess of the d'Urbervilles** and **Anything Goes.** Next, he was cast in a TV film, which was quickly followed by the 2004 movie version of **Vanity Fair.** Unfortunately, his scenes were cut. Boo! But he did appear on the DVD version. **Hurray!**

Robert was then given the chance to audition for the part of perfect prefect Cedric Diggory in the movie **Harry Potter and the Goblet of Fire** (2005). And the casting department obviously knew star material when they saw it because...

HE GOT THE PART.

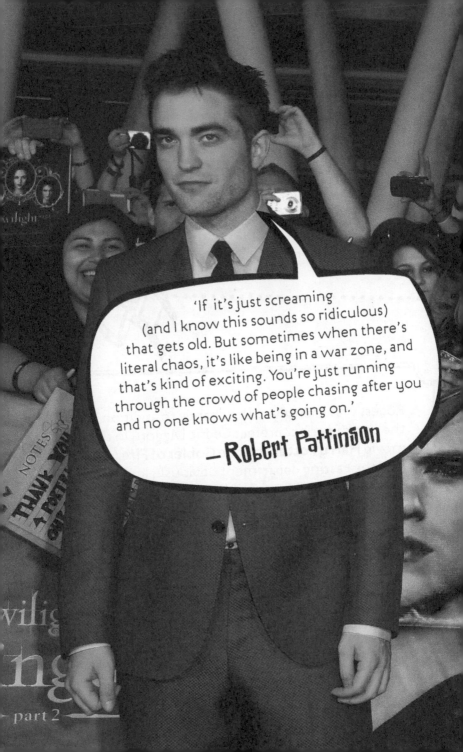

RPattz was born on 13 May, which makes him a **Taurus**. According to astrologers, this means that he is patient, loving, determined and calm. (How lovely!) But he is also jealous, resentful and greedy … (Oh dear.)

Taureans are most likely to get on with those born under the star signs of **Capricorn** and **Virgo**.

But he'll also get along well with **Gemini**, **Cancer**, **Pisces** and **Aries**.

DOES THAT MEAN YOU?

☆ BONUS FACT!

RPattz shares a birthday with the author's grandad. Yes, **REALLY**. And Prince Carl Philip of Sweden. And actor Harvey Keitel. So 13 May is officially a very good day to have a birthday.

FACT.

ROBERT PATTINSON

full name:
Robert Douglas
Thomas Pattinson

Date of birth: 13 May 1986

Place of birth: London, UK

Height: 185cm (6 feet, 1 inch)

Eye colour: Blue-grey (unless he's being a vampire)

Hair colour: Dark brown

Favourite colour: Grey

Favourite clothes: Baseball cap, jeans and leather jacket

Twitter name: Robert Pattinson doesn't have his own Twitter feed, but his fans do! Two of the most popular are **@RobPattzNews** and **@RPLife**.

DAD, Richard

MUM, Clare

Richard Pattinson imports vintage cars. He's the one who encouraged Robert to be an actor, which means he deserves an **ENORMOUS** round of applause. Richard often sends his son top tips on how to be the perfect gentleman. So that's why RPattz is so polite!

Clare Pattinson used to work for a modelling agency. Now, she jets off to afterparties like the huge bash for **Breaking Dawn – Part 2** in November 2012.

OLDER SISTER, Lizzy

EVEN OLDER SISTER, Victoria

Lizzy Pattinson is a celebrity in her own right. She sings with the band Aurora and has made it into the charts on **BOTH** sides of the Atlantic. She's also recorded vocals for the **Twilight** movies.

Victoria is an internet, entrepreneurship, media and social-enterprise enthusiast. And a company director. But when she's not working hard, she goes to celebrity events with her sister, Lizzy.

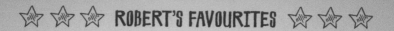
ROBERT'S ACTUAL FAVOURITE THINGS!

Drink:
Diet Coke

Dinosaur:
Diplodocus

Time lord:
Dr Who

 Food:
Cinnamon
Toast Crunch

Actors:
Jack Nicholson
& Marlon Brando

**Comic
book heroes:**
Spider-man,
Batman & X-Men

Football club:
Arsenal FC

Fantasy superpower:
the ability to fly.
(Being able to fly in real life would
make things SO much easier.)

TV show:
The X Factor

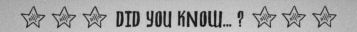
He hates crossing the road; he's terrified of being knocked over.

Robert learnt ballet until the age of 10.

Toy manufacturers have made an action figure of Robert Pattinson dressed as Edward Cullen from the **Twilight** movies. Go on, put it on your Christmas list. You know you want to!

He likes to play darts.

Robert used to do a newspaper round. He doesn't any more, though. He's far too busy being a movie star.

IT WAS ROBERT PATTINSON'S ROLE IN **HARRY POTTER AND THE GOBLET OF FIRE** THAT FIRST MADE HIM FAMOUS. BUT WHAT WOULD HE DO NEXT? HE WANTED TO ACT IN SMALLER FILMS, BUT ALTHOUGH HE DID GET A PART IN A BBC THRILLER CALLED **THE HAUNTED AIRMAN** (2005), HE COULDN'T REALLY FIND ANYTHING ELSE HE WANTED TO DO. HE WAS ABOUT TO QUIT ACTING (GASP!) WHEN SOMETHING REALLY QUITE SPECIAL CAME UP. AND THAT WAS, OF COURSE...

(Imagine a really big DRUMROLL here.)

...TWILIGHT.

(In case you're one of the three people on the entire planet who hasn't heard of **Twilight**, this is the first book in a world-famous vampire romance series written by Stephenie Meyer.)

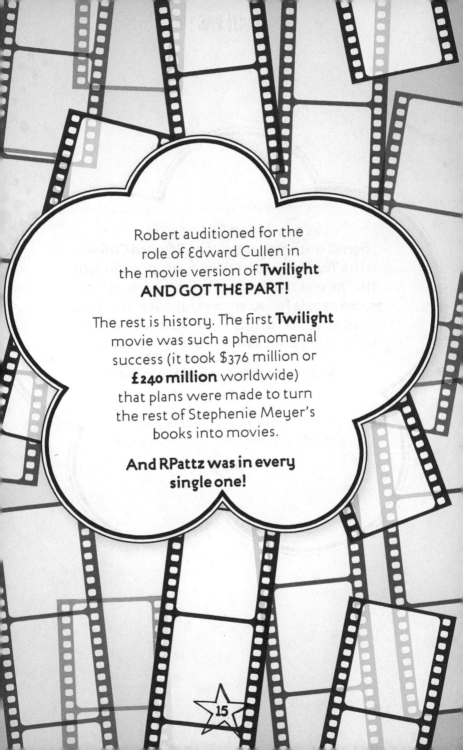

Robert auditioned for the role of Edward Cullen in the movie version of **Twilight AND GOT THE PART!**

The rest is history. The first **Twilight** movie was such a phenomenal success (it took $376 million or **£240 million** worldwide) that plans were made to turn the rest of Stephenie Meyer's books into movies.

And RPattz was in every single one!

When Robert Pattinson first
signed up to play the role of **Edward Cullen**
in the **Twilight** movies, not everyone thought
that he was the right actor for the job. In fact,
75,000 people felt so strongly about it that they
signed a petition asking for someone else to play
the most famous vampire of the 21st century!

**Robert wasn't ditched from the
movie, of course.**

And those 75,000 people have
probably changed their minds now.

;—)

'This thing with everyone knowing you, it's weird, because people have this one-sided relationship where they look at your picture and feel they know you more than someone they actually know. I don't really know myself that well.'

— Robert Pattinson

Which of these films
HASN'T RPattz starred in?

Twilight

Harry Potter
and the Order of
the Phoenix

The Haunted
Airman

Remember
Me

Harry Potter
and the Goblet
of Fire

Water for
Elephants

Harry Potter and the Philosopher's Stone

Stardust

Moon

Like Water for Chocolate

Harry Potter and the Prisoner of Azkaban

All answers on pages 90-93

HARRY POTTER AND THE GOBLET OF FIRE (2005)

WHO'S IN IT?

Daniel Radcliffe ... Harry Potter

Emma Watson ... Hermione Granger

Rupert Grint ... Ron Weasley

Robert Pattinson ... Cedric Diggory

Timothy Spall ... Peter Pettigrew / Wormtail

Michael Gambon ... Albus Dumbledore

Ralph Fiennes ... Lord Voldemort

AND pretty much every other fabulous actor alive today. But if we listed them all, there wouldn't be room for any more fabulous facts about RPattz in this book, which would be a shame.

WHAT SORT OF MOVIE IS IT?

Fantasy adventure

★★★★★

WHERE IS THE MOVIE SET?

Hogwarts School of Witchcraft and Wizardry

★★★★★

WHAT'S IT ABOUT?

This is the fourth of the movie versions of JK Rowling's HUGELY successful books. Set in **Harry Potter's** fourth year at Hogwarts, the Goblet of Fire chooses who will take part in the Triwizard Tournament. The four contestants are Harry Potter, Viktor Krum, Fleur Delacour and **Cedric Diggory** (a prefect, top **Quidditch** player and all-round good guy). Who will win? And who will lose...?

DID YOU KNOW...?

Robert spent three weeks learning to scuba dive for the role of **Cedric Diggory**, because some of his scenes were underwater.

★★★★★

He's still friends with **Stanislav Ianevski**, who played Viktor Krum, his opponent in the Triwizard Tournament.

★★★★★

Cedric Diggory appeared only briefly in **Harry Potter and the Order of the Phoenix** because — um, sorry. That would be telling. You'll have to watch it to find out.

22

'What's **NOT** to love about RPattz? He's just so gorgeous, I could look at him all day. He's also an amazingly talented musician and songwriter. He's the whole package.'

— Jade, 14

ROBERT PATTINSON HAS SOME **VERY** DEDICATED FANS. AND RIGHTLY SO. HE'S REPORTED TO BE A TOTAL GENTLEMAN. WHEN FANS WANT TO HAVE THEIR PHOTO TAKEN WITH HIM, HE POSES, SMILES AND SAYS THANK YOU AFTERWARDS. HE SIGNS ZILLIONS OF AUTOGRAPHS. AND HE'S **ÜBER-CHARMING** IN TV INTERVIEWS. IN FACT, HE'S SUCH A POLITE YOUNG MAN THAT EVEN YOUR GRANNY WOULD LIKE HIM.

One fan persuaded a Twilight crew member to take her baby onto the set so that it could have its photo taken with RPattz!!

Robert says that he finds it pretty intense when everyone's screaming at him at **movie premieres**. Well, you can't blame him, can you? Pop on a pair of sunglasses, stand on a red carpet and get your friends to **scream** at you. Not as much fun as you might think, hmm?

Breaking your nose once might be considered unlucky. Break it twice and you might be seen as accident-prone. But surely, only a **klutz** could break their nose three times...? Yet that's what RPattz did, playing football.

One fan was so upset when **Kristen Stewart** and **Robert Pattinson** split up in 2012 that she posted a clip on **YouTube** about it. The clip went viral and had three million hits. And then Kristen and Robert got back together, only to break up again later!

UNSCRAMBLE
THE LETTERS TO FIND
THE FABULOUS ROLES THAT
ROBERT PATTINSON HAS
PLAYED SO FAR.

EGGED OUR ROSY

★★★★★

ALAS VALID ROD

★★★★★

 BUGGY JOT

★★★★★

WHALER STINKY

★★★★★

 DAWDLER UNCLE

26

Now, FOR BONUS POINTS
AND **EXTREME** RPattz KUDOS,
MATCH THE DECODED CHARACTERS
FROM PAGE 26 WITH THE MOVIES
IN WHICH THEY APPEAR!

TWILIGHT

★ ★ ★ ★ ★

BEL AMI

★ ★ ★ ★ ★

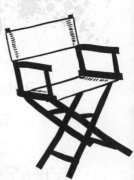

REMEMBER ME

★ ★ ★ ★ ★

THE HAUNTED AIRMAN

★ ★ ★ ★ ★

LITTLE ASHES

All answers on
pages 90-93

TWILIGHT (2008)

WHO'S IN IT?

Kristen Stewart … Bella Swan

Robert Pattinson … Edward Cullen

Taylor Lautner … Jacob Black

WHAT SORT OF MOVIE IS IT?

Fantasy drama romance

★★★★★

WHERE IS THE MOVIE SET?

Forks in Washington, USA (It was actually filmed in Oregon.)

WHAT'S IT ABOUT?

This is the movie version of the first book in Stephenie Meyer's bestselling **Twilight** series. When **Bella Swan** goes to live with her father in Forks – a little town where it seems to rain *all* the time – she doesn't expect to meet someone as totally amazing as **Edward Cullen**. Then she begins to suspect that there is something just a little bit different about him. Especially when he stops a runaway car with just his bare hands. Yikes. What can he be?

★★★★★

DID YOU KNOW... ?

• Robert Pattinson learnt to drive in just **10 HOURS** on the set of **Twilight**. But he says that he's a terrible driver. (So maybe 10 hours wasn't quite long enough.)

• The **Twilight** series of books has sold over 100 million copies worldwide!

Robert Pattinson wore contact lenses when he was filming the **Twilight** movies – not to improve his eyesight, but to make him look more like a vampire. The coloured contact lenses turned his blue-grey human eyes into orange-gold vampire eyes. (Well, have you **EVER** seen a vampire with blue or grey eyes...? **Exactly**.)

The problem was that RPattz hated wearing contact lenses and wasn't terribly good at putting them in.

In fact, he was hopeless at it. So every single time he wore contact lenses – which was pretty much every day he was on set – it took a team of people to put them in. That's two to hold him down and another to do the deed.

When his co-star **Kristen Stewart** had to wear the deadly orange lenses too, Robert was said to be delighted, because at last she'd know what he was going through!

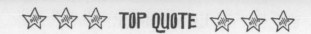

'I hope [fame] hasn't really changed me at all. I don't feel like it has. I don't feel any different than I did before. I guess my friends would have to judge me. But I don't think that I feel any different.'

— Robert Pattinson

ROBERT PATTINSON ISN'T
THE ONLY CELEBRITY TO COME
FROM BARNES IN LONDON. OTHER
FAMOUS NEIGHBOURS, PAST AND
PRESENT, INCLUDE...

Roger McGough
– top children's
poet and author

Dodie Smith –
author of The
Hundred and One
Dalmations

Brian May, Freddie
Mercury and Roger
Taylor — from rock
band Queen

Honor Blackman —
actress who starred
in one of the very
first Bond films!

Alistair McGowan
— comedian and
impressionist

33

Q What do Robert Pattinson and a candle have in common?

A *They're both made of wax!*

NOT THE **REAL** RPATTZ, OF COURSE.
THAT WOULD BE SILLY BECAUSE HE'S PROPER
FLESH AND BLOOD. (UNLESS HE'S BEING
A VAMPIRE, OBVIOUSLY. THEN HE'S A
CENTURY-OLD, **BLOOD-SUCKING MONSTER**.)
NO, WHAT WE'RE TALKING ABOUT HERE
ARE THE WAX DUMMIES AT MADAME
TUSSAUD'S WAXWORK MUSEUMS
AROUND THE WORLD.

When a star has their very own waxwork
dummy – which is basically a pretty life-like
shop dummy – they know they've made it.
They are properly famous!

★★★★★

And Robert Pattinson's waxwork dummy was
unveiled at **Madame Tussaud's** in **Blackpool**,
UK in 2012, with a gang of bouncers to stop fans
getting overexcited and damaging the dummy.
Next, Robert Pattinson's waxwork went on a
world tour of other Madame Tussaud's museums.

YES, YES. HE'S
OFFICIALLY ROBERT PATTINSON.
BUT HE HAS A LOT OF NICKNAMES
TOO. AND SO DO THE PEOPLE
AROUND HIM. HERE ARE JUST
A FEW OF THEM...

Rob

This is what Robert Pattinson's
family and best mates call him.
As do quite a lot of his fans. (It's
short for Robert, obviously.)
Unless, of course, they're
calling him...

...Patty!

This is another
nickname that only
his **BFFs** use.

RPattz

See what the fans did there? They shortened Robert to R and Pattinson to Pattz, put them together and ta-daaaaa... RPattz. **Genius**.

KStew

Robert's **Twilight** co-star and past girlfriend is **Kristen Stewart**. So fans shortened her name too. Try shortening your name in the same way. You might like it! (Or not.)

Twi-hards

These are fans of the **Twilight** movies. They're die-hard fans, you see. A die-hard is someone who supports what they love no matter what. And what do you get if you cross **Twilight** with die-hard? Twi-hard, of course. ;-)

As we know, RPattz
was born on 13 May 1986,
which means that according to
the Chinese zodiac he's a

TIGER!

Do you share the same
sign of the **Chinese zodiac**
with your idol?

★★★★★

Psst. If you know any grown-ups who are RPattz
fans, find out when they're born too. Anyone
born between these dates is a **Tiger** too...

23 January 1974 – 10 February 1975
5 February 1962 – 24 January 1963

FIND YOUR DATE OF BIRTH HERE TO FIND WHICH SIGN OF THE **Chinese Zodiac** YOU ARE.

OX

8 February 1997 –
27 January 1998

TIGER

28 January 1998 –
15 February 1999

RABBIT

16 February 1999 –
4 February 2000

DRAGON

5 February 2000 –
23 January 2001

SNAKE

24 January 2001 –
11 February 2002

HORSE

12 February 2002 –
31 January 2003

GOAT

1 February 2003 –
21 January 2004

MONKEY

22 January 2004 –
8 February 2005

ROOSTER

9 February 2005 –
28 January 2006

NEW MOON (2009)
....
ECLIPSE (2010)

WHO'S IN THESE MOVIES?

Kristen Stewart ... Bella Swan

Robert Pattinson ... Edward Cullen

Taylor Lautner ... Jacob Black

Anna Kendrick ... Jessica

WHAT SORT OF MOVIES ARE THESE?

Fantasy drama romance

WHERE ARE THEY SET?

Forks and Seattle in Washington, USA

WHAT ARE THEY ABOUT?

These are movie versions of the second and third books in Stephanie Meyer's bestselling **Twilight** series. Without revealing any terrible plot spoilers, both **New Moon** and **Eclipse** are all about the romance between Bella and Edward. Oh, and there's Jacob, who quite likes Bella too. And there are LOTS of vampires. And werewolves.

DID YOU KNOW...?

• Robert Pattinson's favourite book of the entire **Twilight** series is ... **New Moon**.
• His trademark über-thick eyebrows were waxed for **Twilight**, but he refused for **New Moon** and **Eclipse**, so if you think they look a bit bushier in the later films, that's the reason why.
• It's rumoured that RPattz's muscles might have been digitally enhanced for **New Moon**. Either that or he spent a lot of time in the gym!

ROBERT IS NOT JUST AN AMAZING ACTOR, YOU KNOW. HE IS ALSO A **MUSICIAN**. IN FACT, HE ALWAYS THOUGHT HE'D END UP WORKING IN MUSIC FOR A LIVING. UNFORTUNATELY, ROBERT'S HAD TO SWAP HIS DREAMS OF PLAYING THE PIANO FOR A MULTI-MILLION DOLLAR CAREER AS ONE OF THE MOST FAMOUS ACTORS IN THE WORLD. OH WELL. YOU WIN SOME, YOU LOSE SOME!

Not only does he sing and play the piano and the guitar, he composes his own music too.

YES, REALLY.

He co-wrote **Never Think**, which features in the original **Twilight** movie. And he sang both that track and **Let Me Sign**. The next time you watch the film, listen out for these – he's not just a pretty (awesome) face, you know.

★★★★★

Twilight director Catherine Hardwicke found the songs so touching that they made her cry. **Awww**.

★★★★★

Robert started playing the **guitar** when he was very young. First, he played classical guitar, but later he swapped to blues.

★★★★★

It's rumoured that **Kristen Stewart** treated RPattz to two very old and very rare guitars for Christmas in 2012 – a 1959 Fender Jazzmaster and a 1947 K&F Lap Steel. Wow.

★★★★★

When he flew to Australia to shoot the movie **The Rover (2013)**, Robert was allowed to take a guitar on the flight, even though it was totally the wrong shape for hand luggage.

Ah, the perks of being a movie star...

43

SO, WHAT SORT OF MUSIC DOES RPATTZ LIKE TO LISTEN TO WHEN HE'S NOT ACTING?

WELL, HE LIKES HIP HOP AND RAP. HE ACTUALLY DREAMED OF BEING A RAPPER WHEN HE WAS YOUNG. HE LIKES A LOT OF OLD BLUES MUSIC. HE **LOVES** VAN MORRISON. HERE ARE A FEW MORE OF HIS FAVOURITE MUSICIANS...

Johnny Flynn

Terry Reed

John Lee Hooker

Eminem

Marcus Foster

Laura Marlin

Wu-Tang Clan

Kings of Leon

Elmore James

When Robert Pattinson is being a musician instead of an actor he calls himself something completely different. He is **Bobby Dupea**!

This isn't some **random name** that he came up with after pulling letters out of a hat. It's actually the name of Oscar-winning actor Jack Nicholson's character in the 1970 film **Five Easy Pieces**. In the movie, Bobby Dupea works as a pianist, something that Robert has always wanted to do. In fact, he says that if acting doesn't work out for him, he might be a pianist anyway!

Unmix the letters of these 10 bizarre movie titles to find Robert Pattinson's real-life movies hidden there!

LIGHT WIT

MEMBER REEM

★★★★★

OMEN NOW

★★★★★

PIC ELSE

WINDBREAK NAG: EARN POT

★★★★★

SPRAWLER OF THE NEAT

★★★★★

SCOOPS LIMO

★★★★★

A MARINATED HEN HUT

★★★★★

BAKE AND WRING: WART TOP

★★★★★

ERR VET HO

47

All answers on pages 90-93

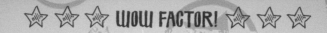
Ever wondered which of the **Twilight** films was the most successful at the cinema? Wonder no more! Here are the official worldwide box office totals for all five fab films...

1. Breaking Dawn – Part 2 $844 (£539) million

2. Breaking Dawn – Part 1 $726 (£464) million

3. New Moon $723 (£462) million

4. Eclipse $712 (£455) million

5. Twilight $376 (£255) million

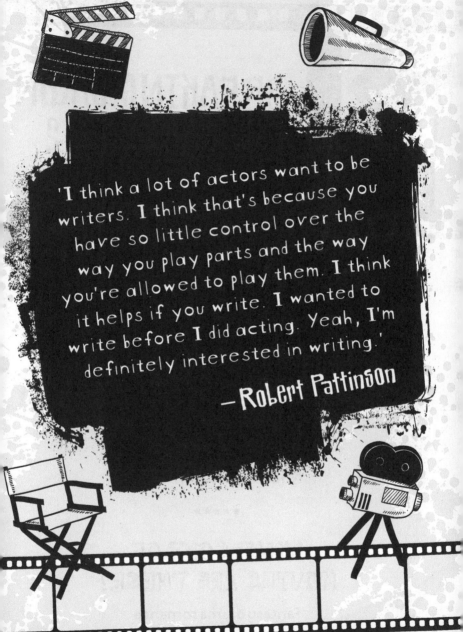

'I think a lot of actors want to be writers. I think that's because you have so little control over the way you play parts and the way you're allowed to play them. I think it helps if you write. I wanted to write before I did acting. Yeah, I'm definitely interested in writing.'

—Robert Pattinson

BREAKING DAWN – PARTS 1 & 2

WHO'S IN THESE MOVIES?

Kristen Stewart … Bella Swan

Robert Pattinson … Edward Cullen

Taylor Lautner … Jacob Black

Billy Burke … Charlie Swan

Anna Kendrick … Jessica

Michael Sheen … Aro

★★★★★

WHAT SORT OF MOVIES ARE THESE?

Fantasy drama romance

WHERE ARE THEY SET?

Forks in Washington, USA and an island off the coast of Brazil. (But they were filmed in Brazil, the USA and Canada.)

★★★★★

WHAT ARE THEY ABOUT?

Such a lot happens in **Breaking Dawn** – the final book of Stephenie Meyer's **Twilight** series – that the movie-makers split it into two parts. So what's it about? Well, the thing is that revealing absolutely **ANYTHING** about either of these movies would spoil the first three. Just in case you haven't seen them. But what we can reveal is that it's all getting **VERY** complicated in Forks. And once again, there are plenty of vampires and werewolves. To find out any more, you'll just have to watch them or read the books.

DID YOU KNOW?

• Stephenie Meyer, the actual author of the **Twilight** series, has a cameo in **Breaking Dawn – Part 1**. She appears when— Oh, that would be telling. Sorry!

• **Breaking Dawn – Parts 1** and **2** were filmed together. It took just over five months to shoot both movies.

• Robert Pattinson learnt how to drive a speedboat for **Breaking Dawn – Part 1**. He crashed it. **Twice**.

• The aftershow party for the very last film in the series was **WILDLY EXTRAVANGANT**. The lucky guests were served by waiters and waitresses dressed as Volturi, before they visited **Twilight** movie locations, like Bella and Edward's meadow, Bella's truck and the Forks High prom! **OK** ... these were smaller versions of the locations, because it's a bit difficult to transport an entire meadow across the USA. But the wolves were definitely not fake. Yikes!

'I liked RPattz in
Harry Potter (Cedric, sob!),
but when he exploded onto the
screen in Twilight, I just fell in love
completely. He's an awesome actor.
It's great when they do that glittery
thing with his skin when he's a vampire
in the sun, but for me they needn't
have bothered with the CGI because
I think he sparkles already.'

— Elektra, 15

So you think you know Robert Pattinson's full name? But do you really know all of it? Which is RPattz's real full name in the list below?

ROBERT FREDERICK THOMAS PATTINSON

★★★★★

DOUGLAS ROBERT THOMAS PATTINSON

★★★★★

ROBERT DOUGLAS THOMAS PATTINSON

★★★★★

ROBERT DOUGLAS BERNARD PATTINSON

★★★★★

ROBERT DOUGLAS PATTINSON THOMAS

All answers on pages 90-93

Robert Pattinson might be able to jump from the top of waterfalls, scale trees and run faster than a bullet in the **Twilight** movies, but in real life he's not very athletic.

SERIOUSLY.

He admits that running doesn't come naturally to him, and says he didn't enjoy the flying sequences in the **Twilight** movies because the harness he had to wear was **VERY** uncomfortable and he had to run at the same time. Good job he had a stuntman, eh?

REMEMBER ME (2010)

WHO'S IN IT?

Robert Pattinson … Tyler Hawkins

Emilie de Ravin … Ally Craig

Pierce Brosnan … Charles Hawkins

Chris Cooper … Neil Craig

WHAT SORT OF MOVIE IS IT?

Romantic drama

★★★★★

WHERE IS THE MOVIE SET?

New York City, USA

WHAT'S IT ABOUT?

Robert Pattinson plays **Tyler Hawkins**, a university student whose parents have split up after his brother's death. He doesn't get on well with his father. And he's always getting in trouble with the police ... until he meets a girl called Ally.

DID YOU KNOW... ?

• While taking a break from filming on location in **New York City**, an overexcited fan and a bunch of paparazzi ran after Robert. He took to his heels and ran ... straight into a parked car. Ooops. (Don't worry. He was fine.)

'I keep forgetting that I'm speaking in an American accent sometimes. The dangerous thing is that you end up forgetting what your real accent is after a while... It's really strange; I've never done a job in an American accent before... I grew up watching American movies and stuff and I kind of learned how to act ... from American films.'

— Robert Pattinson

You won't be surprised to hear that the super-talented RPattz has been nominated for a lot of awards. (He's won quite a few, too...)

2008

WON

the New Hollywood award in the **Hollywood Film Awards**.

★★★★★

2009

NOMINATED

for Best Newcomer award in the **Empire Awards**.

WON

the Choice Hottie (Male) and Choice Move Actor awards at the **Teen Choice Awards**.

59

2010

WON

the Hollywood's Most Influential Top Unexpected Musicians award.

the Choice Movie Actor award at the **Teen Choice Awards**.

One of **TIME** magazine's 100 **Most Influential People in the World**

Number 50 in Forbes' **Celebrity 100**.

NOMINATED

for Best Actor award in the **Empire Awards**.

★★★★★

2011

WON

the Choice Movie Actor and Choice Vampire awards at the **Teen Choice Awards**.

2013

NOMINATED

for the Best Actor in a
Canadian Film award by the
Vancouver Film Critics Circle.

★★★★★

FIGHT!

In 2009 and 2011, Robert Pattinson won the
MTV Movie Award for Best Fight, which he
shared with Bryce Dallas Howard (Victoria),
Xavier Samuel (Riley) and Cam Gigandet
(James). They weren't real fights, obviously
– just very good pretend fights. (Probably.)

★★★★★

KISS!

Finally, in 2009, 2010, 2011 **AND** 2012,
Robert Pattinson shared the MTV
Movie Award for Best Kiss with Kristen
Stewart, his co-star in the **Twilight** saga
and on-off girlfriend in real life.

In 2012, Robert Pattinson fell in love ... with an abandoned puppy who was living in a dog pound in Louisiana, **USA**. There was no time to lose – the dog was just **ONE DAY** away from being put to sleep. Kind-hearted Robert adopted the dog, flew him on a private jet to Los Angeles and the two have been together ever since.

He named the black and tan dog 'Bear'.

Awww.

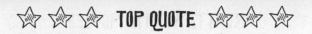

'I wanted to play piano in restaurants in the south of France. I went there on holiday once and I saw this guy playing in an old tuxedo ... I thought that was the coolest thing. So what's happened to me with **Twilight** isn't really what I'd planned.'

— Robert Pattinson

WATER FOR ELEPHANTS (2011)

WHO'S IN IT?

Reese Witherspoon ... Marlena

Robert Pattinson ... Jacob Jankowski

Christoph Waltz ... August

Paul Schneider ... Charlie

Hal Holbrook ... Old Jacob

WHAT SORT OF MOVIE IS IT?

Romantic drama

★★★★★

WHERE IS THE MOVIE SET?

1930s and present-day USA

WHAT'S IT ABOUT?

When veterinary student **Jacob Jankowski** finds out that his parents have died, that's not the only bad news. It turns out that his parents had **huge debts** and he's now penniless. He drops out of college and hitches a ride on a train. Except, it's not any old train. It belongs to the Benzini Brothers Most Spectacular Show on Earth. It's a **circus train**. And on board is an elephant called Rosie.

★★★★★

DID YOU KNOW... ?

• **Channing Tatum** and **Andrew Garfield** also auditioned for the role of Jacob. They didn't get it, obviously.

• This wasn't the first time that Robert Pattinson had acted with **Reese Witherspoon**. They both appeared in **Vanity Fair** (2004), but Robert's scenes were cut from the final movie. GASP!

'RPattz is totally gorgeous! My room is covered with his posters, especially of him in *Twilight*. I've seen that film, like a hundred times. It would be amazing to meet him one day, but I worry that I might faint if I ever did, even though I dream about it happening.'
— Cassie, 15

RPattz

Reese Witherspoon

Um... you see... the thing is that RPattz – sorry, **ROBERT PATTINSON** – doesn't actually LIKE being called RPattz. In fact, RPattz – we mean, **ROBERT PATTINSON** – would like to find the person who came up with the nickname and... Well, we won't go there, OK? Let's just say that RPattz – oops, done it again, **ROBERT PATTINSON** – doesn't want to shake their hand and say, 'Hey, thanks for coming up with an awesome nickname that millions of people around the world instantly recognise.' Nope. Not keen.

'Cosmopolis is a game-changer for [Robert Pattinson]. He's distant, sardonic, nihilistic, enigmatic and very watchable... Cronenberg [the director] has helped lift another level of performance from Pattinson, who channels his vampiric blankness for deeper purposes...'

Rob James, Total Film

'One minute he was a complete unknown. And then, out of a clear blue sky, *Twilight* happened, and he turned into Elvis. Girls on every continent went bananas...'

Sanjiv Bhattacharya, The Observer

'I think he's made really smart choices. He has a deep desire to earn the status he has, and [*Water for Elephants* **and** *Cosmopolis*] both have hardcore directors and quality material. I think it speaks more to who Rob is than the *Twilight* series, because he comes from a literary background. He shows up to set reading Molière.'

Wyck Godfrey, Twilight producer

'He comes to set with no expectations or attitude, none of those things you worry someone of his level of fame is going to have.'

Christina Ricci, co-star in Bel Ami

'I think Robert has been very clever in the way that he has tried to branch out and do lots of other different things… He seems to have a good head on his shoulders.'

Michael Sheen, co-star in the Twilight movies

THE ROVER (2013)

WHO'S IN IT?

Guy Pearce ... Eric

Robert Pattinson ... Reynolds

Scoot McNairy... Henry

Nash Edgerton ... Soldier

Samuel F. Lee... Acrobat

★★★★★

WHAT SORT OF MOVIE IS IT?

A modern Western

WHERE IS THE MOVIE SET?

The Australian Desert, in a not-particularly
nice sort of future

WHAT'S IT ABOUT?

The film is due for release soon. Behind-the-scenes gossip reveals that **The Rover** is about an Australian called Eric (played by Guy Pearce) who runs into a whole heap of trouble with a gang and loses **EVERYTHING**. Naturally, he wants it back. So he gets Reynolds – an ex-gang member – to help him. Who's Reynolds? Our RPattz, of course.

★★★★★

DID YOU KNOW... ?

Robert struggled with the heat, sweat, dirt and flies during filming. But who can blame him? The **Australian Desert** (with sometime temperatures of 50°C) is a TINY bit hotter than RPattz's hometown of Barnes! He had his hair cut **really short*** for the role and he wore **teeth make up** to make his pearly whites look super-dirty.

*It'll grow again, don't worry!

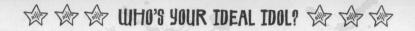

WHICH ROBERT PATTINSON CHARACTER WOULD **YOU** GET ALONG WITH BEST? ANSWER THESE MULTIPLE-CHOICE QUESTIONS AND THEN TURN TO PAGES 90-93 TO FIND YOUR IDEAL MATCH...

1. What's your favourite hobby...?

a Looking after animals

b Painting

c Sprinting and jumping

d Being an all-round nice guy

2. Which stunt makes you say WOW...?

a Flying

b Spending a very, very long time underwater

c Jumping onto a moving train

d Brushstrokes

3. Does your ideal Robert Pattinson character have...?

a A beautifully curled moustache

b Orange eyes

c A strong sense of justice

d An encyclopaedic knowledge of animals

4. What sort of personality do you most admire...?

a Very, very, very intense

b Polite and gentlemanly

c Shy

d Eccentric

73

All answers on pages 90-93

HOW WELL DO **YOU** KNOW ROBERT PATTINSON? TRY YOUR LUCK WITH THIS TOTALLY TRICKY TRIVIA QUIZ AND FIND OUT...

1. Which instruments does Robert Pattinson play...?

a The piano and the harp

b The piano and the guitar

c The guitar and the tenor saxophone

d The piano and the triangle

2. Which one of these things has Robert Pattinson NOT learnt how to do for one of his film roles...?

a Play baseball

b Play darts

c Scuba-dive

d Drive

3. Which of these activities is Robert Pattinson REALLY good at doing…?

a Driving a car

b Operating a speedboat

c Running

d Playing the guitar

4. What is Robert Pattinson's favourite look when he's not on set…?

a Tuxedo

b Onesie

c Polo shirt and shorts

d Baseball cap, jeans and leather jacket

5. Which of Robert Pattinson's co-stars is also his on-off girlfriend...?

a Reese Witherspoon

b Kristen Stewart

c Kristin Scott Thomas

d Juliette Binoche

6. Which musician does Robert Pattinson absolutely LOVE...?

a Van Morrison

b Alanis Morissette

c David Van Day

d Olly Murs

7. Which of these features does Robert Pattinson NOT have...?

a Blue-grey eyes

b A tattoo

c Wild hair (unless he's just been to the barber and it's very, very short and well-behaved)

d Bushy eyebrows

8. What did Robert Pattinson take onto a plane as hand luggage...?

a A parrot

b His very own red carpet, so he could roll it out wherever he went

c A year's supply of Cinnamon Toast Crunch

d A guitar

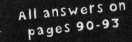
All answers on pages 90-93

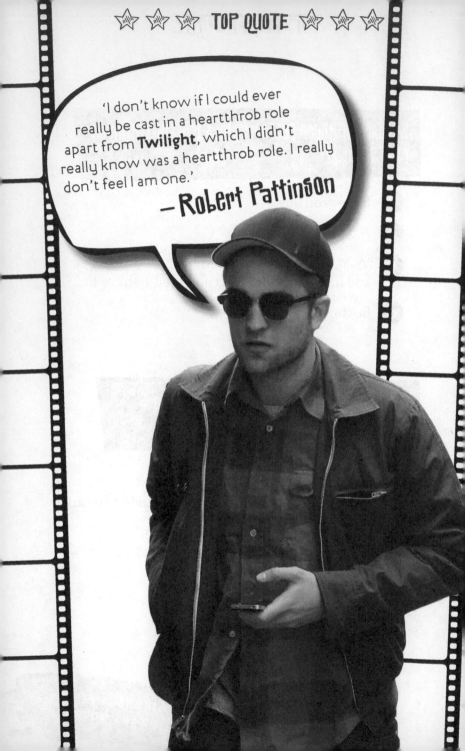

'I don't know if I could ever really be cast in a heartthrob role apart from **Twilight**, which I didn't really know was a heartthrob role. I really don't feel I am one.'

— Robert Pattinson

Robert Pattinson may have once starred in a magazine feature with two armfuls of scribbled 'tattoos'. But that's all they were – just scribbles. Because RPattz has **NO TATTOOS** in real life.

Not a big eagle with its wings spread across his back.

Not his girlfriend's name on his arm.

Not a single one.

So, you've read the book and soaked up the facts. Do you know your idol now? Check out this **MEGA-QUIZ** to find out if you're a true RPattz fan. There are three parts to test your knowledge to the max.

1 What are Robert Pattinson's sisters called?

2 He once appeared in the stage production of a Thomas Hardy novel. Which one?

3 Where is his 2010 movie Remember Me **set**?

4 How tall is he?

5 When is his birthday?

6 Which football team does he support?

7 What part-time job did he have when he was young?

8 Which two Harry Potter films did Robert appear in?

9 Who wrote the original Twilight **series on which the five movies were based?**

10 What colour contact lenses does he **wear in** Twilight**?**

Were your answers **FAN**-tastic? Go to pages 90-93 to find out! And if you're up for a challenge, turn the page for the rest of **THE BIG QUIZ**. But beware – it's for true fans only ...

11 Which actor most inspires him?

12 How many people auditioned for the part of Edward Cullen?

13 Which two types of supernatural creatures appear in the Twilight books and movies?

14 What is the name of the elephant in Water for Elephants?

15 Who is his favourite time lord?

16 What sort of dancing did he learn until the age of 10?

17 Which sign of the Chinese zodiac is he?

18 Which Spanish surrealist painter did he play in the movie *Little Ashes*?

19 What is his favourite food?

20 Does RPattz like being called RPattz?

21 What is the name of Robert Pattinson's dog?

22 Is he good at putting in contact lenses?

23 Which name does he call himself when he's being a musician?

24 What did he have to learn to do to play the part of Cedric Diggory in Harry Potter and the Goblet of Fire?

25 Can you list the Twilight films, in order of release?

26 Which Twilight **film was the most successful at the box office?**

27 Which song did he both co-write and sing for the original Twilight soundtrack?

28 How long did it take him to learn to drive?

29 What's his favourite dinosaur?

30 What is his back-up plan for a career if the acting doesn't work out?

All answers on pages 90-93

These are the movies that RPattz has appeared in:

Curse of the Ring (2004) TV movie
Giselher

★★★★★

Harry Potter and the Goblet of Fire (2005)
Cedric Diggory

★★★★★

The Haunted Airman (2006) TV movie
Toby Jugg

★★★★★

The Bad Mother's Handbook (2007) TV movie
Daniel Gale

★★★★★

How to Be (2008)
Art

★★★★★

Little Ashes (2008)
Salvador Dalí

★★★★★

Twilight (2008)
Edward Cullen

★★★★★

The Summer House (2009) Short film
Richard

New Moon (2009)
Edward Cullen

★★★★★

Remember Me (2010)
Tyler Hawkins

★★★★★

Eclipse (2010)
Edward Cullen

★★★★★

Water for Elephants (2011)
Jacob

★★★★★

Breaking Dawn – part 1 (2011)
Edward Cullen

★★★★★

Bel Ami (2012)
Georges Duroy

★★★★★

Cosmopolis (2012)
Eric Packer

★★★★★

Breaking Dawn – part 2 (2012)
Edward Cullen

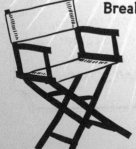

★★★★★

The Rover (2013)
Reynolds

SINCE THE **TWILIGHT** MOVIES,
RPATTZ HAS SWITCHED TO ACTING IN
FILMS MADE BY INDEPENDENT COMPANIES,
SUCH AS **BEL AMI** AND **COSMOPOLIS**.
HE STARRED AS SPANISH SURREALIST
PAINTER SALVADOR DALÍ IN A MOVIE
CALLED **LITTLE ASHES**, TOO.

Whether it was because of the orange contact lenses or just because he fancied a break from being a vampire, since the Twilight **movies, RPattz has had a complete break from being a blood-sucking heartthrob. He's been a French scoundrel, a 1920s billionaire, a Spanish painter and most recently an Australian cowboy.**

WHAT'S NEXT, WHO KNOWS ...?

But whatever it is, whether it's more movies, perhaps a few more awards, more red carpets or the musical career that he's always said is his back-up plan, it's sure to be **AWESOME**.

SO YOU THINK YOU KNOW
RPATTZ **SO** WELL THAT YOU
COULD RECOGNISE HIM IN
THE DARK ...?

PROVE IT.

Check out the silhouette below and
guess who's who in this photo of
three of the **Twilight** cast.

Then turn over the page to find the answer
to this and all the other quiz questions
dotted throughout the book!

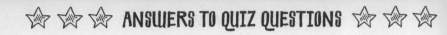

Pages 18-19

FILMS STARRING RPATTZ

TWILIGHT

THE HAUNTED AIRMAN

HARRY POTTER AND THE GOBLET OF FIRE

HARRY POTTER AND THE ORDER OF THE PHOENIX

REMEMBER ME

WATER FOR ELEPHANT

Pages 26-27

MIX AND MATCH

GEORGES DUROY - Bel Ami

SALVADOR DALI - Little Ashes

TOBY JUGG - The Haunted Airman

TYLER HAWKINS - Remember Me

EDWARD CULLEN - Twilight

Pages 46-47

THE MEGAMIX MOVIE QUIZ

TWILIGHT

REMEMBER ME

NEW MOON

ECLIPSE

BREAKING DAWN: PART ONE

WATER FOR ELEPHANTS

COSMOPOLIS

THE HAUNTED AIRMAN

BREAKING DAWN: PART TWO

THE ROVER

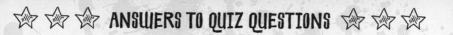

Page 54
STUCK IN THE MIDDLE
ROBERT DOUGLAS
THOMAS PATTINSON

Pages 72–73
WHO'S YOUR IDEAL IDOL?
1 a) Jacob
b) Salvador
c) Edward
d) Cedric

2 a) Edward
b) Cedric
c) Jacob
d) Salvador

3 a) Salvador
b) Edward
c) Cedric
d) Jacob

4 a) Edward
b) Cedric
c) Jacob
d) Salvador

EDWARD CULLEN (**TWILIGHT**)

JACOB (**WATER FOR ELEPHANTS**)

SALVADOR DALÍ (**LITTLE ASHES**)

CEDRIC DIGGORY (**HARRY POTTER**

AND THE GOBLET OF FIRE)

Pages 74–77

TOP TRIVIA QUIZ

1 b) The piano and the guitar
2 b) Play darts
3 d) Playing the guitar
4 d) Baseball cap, jeans
and leather jacket
5 b) Kristen Stewart
6 a) Van Morrison
7 b) A tattoo
8 d) A guitar

Pages 80-81

THE BIG QUIZ

1 Lizzy and Victoria
2 *Tess of the d'Urbervilles*
3 New York City
4 He's 185 cm (6 feet 1 inch) tall
5 13 May
6 Arsenal FC
7 He delivered newspapers
**8 Harry Potter and the Goblet
of Fire** and **Harry Potter and the
Order of the Phoenix**
9 Stephenie Meyer
10 Orange

Pages 82-83
11 Jack Nicholson

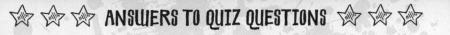

12 3000
13 Vampires and werewolves
14 Rosie
15 Dr Who
16 Ballet
17 Tiger
18 Salvador Dalí
19 Cinnamon Toast Crunch
20 No

Pages 84-85
21 Bear
22 No
23 Bobby Dupea
24 Scuba-dive
25 Twilight, New Moon, Eclipse, Breaking Dawn – Part 1, Breaking Dawn – Part 2
26 Breaking Dawn – Part 2
27 Never Think
28 10 hours
29 Diplodocus
30 He'll be a musician instead

Page 89
WHO'S WHO?
(from left to right) Taylor Lautner, Kristen Stewart and Robert Pattinson

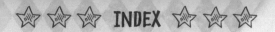

Congratulations!

Now you really, truly **KNOW** your idol
(probably better than his own mum).
But what about your **OTHER** idols, like
One Direction, **Olly Murs**,
Katy Perry, Justin Bieber and
James Arthur?

DON'T PANIC!

Simply check out the other titles
in the series and become an

EVEN BIGGER FAN...

95

Want to Know Your Idol?

TOTALLY AWESOME TITLES IN THE SERIES:

9780750279321

9780750279338

9780750279307

9780750279314

9780750278386

9780750278362

WHY NOT COLLECT THEM ALL?